The energetic voices in *Three Witches' Songs* redefine the meaning of 'witches.' The poems, strongly lyrical in words and rhyme, persuasively ask for women to be free of traditional shackles. Wit and humour are effective tools of social satire used by the poets whose individual and collective vision sweeps over the urban landscape, promising the dream of women's empowerment. Witchery and magic are the new names for positive action and the alternative world of supra-reality offers splendid opportunities for identity formation. —MALASHRI LAL

THREE WITCHES' SONGS

APARNA SINGH
NABANITA SENGUPTA
SUDESHNA CHAKRAVORTY

Hawakal
PUBLISHERS
New Delhi | Calcutta

HAWAKAL
New Delhi | Calcutta

HAWAKAL PUBLISHERS PRIVATE LIMITED
70 B/9 Amritpuri, East of Kailash, New Delhi 65
33/1/2 K B Sarani, Mall Road, Calcutta 80

Email info@hawakal.com
Website www.hawakal.com

Cover designed by Bitan Chakraborty
Illustrations by Abhishek Maity

First edition (paperback) July 2022

ISBN: 978-93-91431-32-7 (paperback)

Price: 500 INR | 15.99 USD

To all those witches who could not be burnt.

FOREWORD

Women talking, women together, women voicing their observations — one can safely say that from time immemorial it all has been frowned upon by a society that is largely patriarchal. Khana had her tongue slashed for correctly predicting the weather much before meteorology became a science. Akka Mahadevi and Lal Ded were viewed with reservation and thought to be 'mad'. Andal was an aberration in her times. Meera Bai was simply not an honourable woman for claiming Krishna to be her lover. Imagine then what happens when women call themselves witches and come together to speak — in poetry. We know how quick one would be, as an uninformed individual, to categorise these women as given to diabolism, or Satanism, or what is commonly called magic and witchcraft. While the truth perhaps is that women were exploring science, society, and their own and others' well-being via logic and language since centuries.

This is why in this book, where three women gather to discuss life and loves, especially in the shadow of Covid-19 pandemic, they call themselves witches and make their voices heard.

Patriarchy has created this fear of women where 'witches' historically are located as errant women pitted against the controlling male. Theology was used to keep the divide — women being on the dark side, in the realm of the absurd and often demoniac, and hence, as the gendered evil enemy of God. While the latter bit has been documented well in the West

— theology, morality texts, demonology, etc. — the Indian society too, particularly in the modern times, has deemed the very notion of 'witches' as moral disruptors and a challenge to the feudal Brahmanical structure in place. The spirit of the oppressive *Malleus Maleficarum* therefore, existed among us for long: women unsupervised are undisciplined, requiring trial and penalty, and so on and so forth. Women are goddess, women are Hidimba, women are also the repository of mysteries such as childbirth, agriculture, cooking, and foresight — all of them change agents. For the male partner stricken with awe and fear, women talking mostly means

> "...a charm of powerful trouble,
> Like a hell-broth boil and bubble."

The three witches in this delightful book of ditties — for these verses are rhymes and songs that flow freely — remind us of what was bountiful before the pandemic struck and what is lost, and yet to be gained back. They talk of bodies, transgression, and the creative lockdown that has been a woman's experience almost exclusively down the ages. To listen to them is liberating.

It is a world now where "Birds — still there —", beats gently yet persistently as a reminder. The articulation, "To read or to unread" is what drives our intellect, the witches chant. Kali, Eve, and the Wife are there to alert the reader that it is not a novel sickness or plague, but the stricken human mind that has long wronged the woman.

We might chuckle at what Arthur Miller had written in *The Crucible* — "Until an hour before the Devil fell, God thought him beautiful in Heaven" We will turn it around from the androcentric tales we've been reading — our beautiful devils, our talking, chatting women are in fact the architects of a heaven, saving it from falling apart.

NABINA DAS
Hyderabad

THE FUN BEGINS

The witches congregated on a beautiful afternoon (or did it happen purely in their minds? who knows? But as a benign headmaster had told to his wizard student — why should anything be less real, simply because it is happening inside our heads). They congregated, and they harmonized, synchronized, toggled and tussled in an *adda* that only they could come up with. They chuckled and raved and ranted and wept and chronicled their tale in songs short and long.

Ayana, Nerissa, and Syrma call themselves Aparna, Nabanita, and Sudeshna in another world. Three different figures with different characteristics, peculiarities, follies, and yet somewhere merging into a whole; (as the song goes — we all call ourselves 'I'), try to break out of the absurd drama of daily existence to give voice to the unexpressed poets in them. They invite you to listen, to laugh, to cry, to rage, to love, and of course to sing along in the following pages.

Ayana and Nerissa often slipped into a garrulous mode, losing track of time. Ayana had so much to say about the world drifting astray, while Nerissa pitched in with her worldly wisdom and deep probings. Syrma, an attentive listener, never missed a beat. She came up with songs that filled in with sensitive imaginative sweeps.

Aparna Singh
Nabanita Sengupta
Sudeshna Chakravorty
Calcutta
June 2022

What follows is a work of poetry-in-fiction
where all characters are not fictional.

PRESENTING

Aparna Singh in and as *Ayana*
Nabanita Sengupta in and as *Nerissa*
Sudeshna Chakravorty in and as *Syrma*

beyond thunder lightning rain
the three witches met again

neither the hills
nor the plains
could match the
sizzling caffeine

chitchats and gossips
wise and juicy
profane and saucy
they poured it all out
the messy and the glossy

the coffee arrived
tumbled out thoughts
unzipped hearts
and unminced words

so many locked down days
order and disarray
and so much to say
oh so much to say

PASSPORT | AYANA

Rummaging past dishevelled sheets of memory
I found an old passport.
The woman somewhat like me looked back
sifting through buoyant dreams.
Those eyes roved world weary escapades building
into joys, sorrows, pains, agonies and smiles...
The passport whispered.
It smelt of limitless skies,
redolent petrichor and fathomless oceans.
Touring back and forth in waves of time
I felt its engulfing turbulence.
Embracing my travel-less placidity it consoled me
with good old bygone days.
It coaxed me into long lost diaries,
punctuated with slippery remembrances.

as the adda gathered steam
stories unimpeded poured in

ARCHIVED | NERISSA

We are
reminiscent yesterdays
upon an embroidered chiffon
that sits coy in a wardrobe corner

A heady smell from past
like an oversized overcoat
wraps the conversations
In the warmth of a wintry tea

through words freshly packed
we dish out old staples
That belonged once to
to the zone of reality

Yet now, in exile
Separated by time,

we speak a language
of déjà-vous
and count the growing age
of memories, waiting
till the gates open once more

the other two sat quiet
heaving a sigh
gates were opening
slow and well nigh

A SONNET OF NEW NORMAL CLICHÈS |

NERISSA *sang on*

Gracias! Beings of new normal
limited exchanges and words formal
bottled desires and unspoken words
limited editions of humans on earth

Blue skies and green plants have failed all around
to rouse interest and sustain a mind sound
Day long chit chats and verses exchanged
they too now gone in a quarantined phase

A numb stillness steadily gaining force
It accepts no lockdown, no closed doors
Viral habit of washing and cleansing
threatens to peel off the skin of being

Masks on mask the new normal cliche
Separated, you live the norm of the day

the three witches pondered
of a life gone awry
their love for travel
all wasted and weary
where did their broomsticks take them last

At Paharpur 2020 | Nerissa

Eloquence dripped in the ruins
and a world from centuries ago
communicated in universal tongue
bringing stories carved in stones
a silence louder than words.
Stories of love and passion
of human values and oppression
unseen blood trickled through
these history, maligned stones.
Admiring, in awe, onlookers
had their own stories too,
mingled in that ancient history,
set in stony silence.
They set off in a quest
as old as these stones!

Tales of human oppression
flow on through ages
and Art lives on
though bruised once and more.

and they kept wondering
of places seen and unseen
beyond their city
and even within
lovingly imagined
yet never been

SEARCH | AYANA

Shadows have lengthened,
They have spread into
Lanes and by-lanes.
Streets, roads and deserts
Closely conspire...
The invisible sky whispers
To the horizons stretched far.
Birds — still there — tweet in unison
Shadows darken into the night.

Even in my city I long for it.
The roads, the lanes, and the sun,
Reclaiming the lost sameness —
Walls, have they acquired colours?
A reluctant palimpsest of fading graffiti
Old names with new tidings
Barely hide the ones unseen.

Immune to the coldness
Of marbled fantasies
Cold winds rip apart
A jumble of facades...
Scaffolding and pitched roofs.

wandering feet now stayed
for months long dismayed
showcases of memories
lovingly displayed

SOUVENIRS | NERISSA

That framed Seshat,
hanging from my wall
was a brother's gift
from his last trip to Nile.

And the Burj Khalifa you see
perching upon the
drawing room shelf
is a gift of a friend
from her first trip overseas...

On the fridge door
a tuktuk shares space
with a South African safari
and an Ajanta dancer
is flanked by Myanmar's Buddha
and Australian reef...
There's much more than this
poem can hold!

Looking around, I find the world
peeping out from nook and corner
of my home

chosen thoughtfully by loving hearts
each a curio of remembrance

Within walls of my home
objects from all around
metamorphose into fairy tales
of kinship, love and affection.

spell books gone stale
in quarantine days
the witches get thinking
in what ways
to get their zing in place

no diagon alley in sight
but college street brings respite
wonderful to amble around
free
and also to visit in memory

DUSK AT COLLEGE STREET | NERISSA

In narrow lanes
float pages freshly baked,
mellowed in the evening light,
dimmed with cobwebs
cosy, perching upon
the erect street lamps.

Within the maze
To read or to unread
remains the moot question.

Hands explore walls,
as they crumble
into elegiac verses
that bear apathies
of a corporated living,
on a fading brick red skin
those fingers etch their prints
upon the falling scales of time
pumping fresh blood
within arteries, spurting
new lease of youth.

From a distance
stars look upon
a rejuvenation
as the dim lit alleys horde
more and more pages
hard or paper bound
adding layers
to be explored
in the maze of
knowledge and ignorance.

in pre-broomstick days
college street meant local trains
where lives chugged on iron wheels

stories soaked in blood and sweat
stories wrapped in smiles and strains
more enchanting than those on reels

A JOURNEY BY LOCAL TRAIN | NERISSA

In a local train
thousand pickled bodies
wiggle their way into
their daily bread.

Morning pickles are less tangy,
unsauced yet in grime
that the whole day holds
and seeps in slowly
through the pores
drip drip
drip drip
into the bones.
Sleepy heads bob up and down
awaiting the jar
of pickled limes
to become soft and juicy
with every passing time.

the train moves from station to next
a relentless pursuit, in a framed time

Evening wafts out strong odour

of daily chores
unmitigated by air-conditioned rooms or plush offices
that calls for an uber ride home,
if not in chauffeured or self-driven goals,
SUVs and their sleek interiors
soft seats and sexy stereos
while bodies in compartments
ooze out their last drops
of strength in a bid to return home

the train moves from station to next
a relentless pursuit, bound in its zone

lives roll on,
station and beyond
in trains bodies float
what floats more
are dreams, hopes
some fulfilled and some
thwarted aspirations

witch Nerissa in garrulous tone
kept the chit chat going on
pensive Syrma still lost
in the days gone past
but this was no time to mourn

Syrma dived her witchy nose
in her fat thick book
fished out oft-told myths
in feminist spices re-cooked

WINGS OF FIRE | SYRMA

Ucarus — yes that's what my father called me —
Born as I was, after an 'illustrious' brother, marked for success since birth.
(and named... as an echo, an 'afterthought').
You have heard of him, p'haps —
He supposedly wanted to fly to the sun —
(or that was what he was told he had to want).
I knew otherwise, though —
He loved the sea, Icarus did.
Would sit for hours on the rocks,
Letting the waves nibble at his toes.

It was I, on the other hand, who eyed the ball of fire.
First, as I played on the dusty roads of my village,
during my all too shrunken childhood.
And then...everyday... I would steal furtive glances at 'him'.

As I rushed about 'caring' for the family
(trying to live up to my name's burden)
Cooking, washing, mending —
As the woman has to, to earn her keep...
I was the one who mended his clothes after my father returned
after building the Minotaur's labyrinth —
Mended the tatters, so that only his glory shone bright;
not his struggles.
I washed up after him too,
The day he took Perdix up to the mountains...
Our bright young cousin,
who showed threatening signs of being as talented
as the wonderful Daedalus...
and hence never returned from that trip
to the mountain top with the hero.
I washed off the tell-tale dirt stains
and brambles from my father's shirt...

And then the duty fell on me, to gather feathers for wings —
For my father wanted Icarus to fly to the sun — my sun!
My brother had to be moulded in the image
of his illustrious parent
The way I remoulded the wax
from used candles into new ones...
Useful, bright but always shorter and less than the original.

I saw Icarus those days — waiting to take the flight
chalked out for him...
Looking wistfully all the time
to the Ocean where his heart lay...

And then the day finally dawned —
Decked up in the wings the obedient daughter,
the sacrificing sister, had glued to apparent perfection...

My brother soared — higher and higher...closer to the fire
As had been 'my' desire...

I run to the ocean, even as her lover slowly disappears
into another's blinding embrace. She is silent. She is still.
But I can hear the roar of her breaking heart.
'May the world be his oyster' — is all that she would say.
She forgives...as a 'good' woman 'supposedly' does...

But...what is this? "Isn't that him?", she suddenly gasps.
Is he struggling? Is he coming back?
Borrowed ambitions have not agreed well with him —
And he comes hurtling down —
Down to certain death or a 'fate worse'— the tag of a failed man.
I whisper to the ocean — and suddenly she smiles...
And opens up her arms for the man
too weak to have defied norms for her...
Ready to shelter him against the world's judgemental stares...
because that is what love does —
As she lets her waves caress over Icarus' ignominy...
I look into the distance.
and see Daedalus...
For once broken...for once beaten...
Wouldn't it have been easier to sew the wings on,
instead of relying on wax that melts?
But whoever thinks of picking a woman's brain for grand ideas?
Before resetting my face into a suitably sympathetic expression,
before setting off to comfort my hapless father...
As a 'good' daughter supposedly would...

Clutching the spiel of unused thread close to my heart,
For a moment I allow myself a victor's smile...

the other two were rapt listeners
of that untold tale
the real and the mythical cleverly dovetailed
women and myths long overdue
to be told from their point of view

KALI | AYANA

Get her dressed
Stressed the purohit
Clothes become women
Goddess or not!
Woman slayer and woman rebel
Assailing his modesty
Infuriating his chastity
Defying propriety
Set his world to unrest.

Gods too were clueless
She eluded their godly designs
Tame her, train her, keep her in control
In unison they chanted.
She gleefully obliged
Tearing, shattering, crushing confines.

Dancing deliriously the dance of death
In rebellious frenzy flouting flaunting
The bruteness of love.
Camouflaging birth in death she took
The unforeseen step...
Crossing those boundaries
That were never meant to be.

songs long overlooked
Nerissa her own versions cooked
to match the ones
already chanted and cooed

EVE'S CHOICE | NERISSA

Choices come with riders
as it did for Eve
with the apple that she chose
in conscious defiance
of a power unseen.

Paradise lost forever
in gained wisdom,
Knowledge brings woes
and fear of comfort bygone
The archetypal mother
Carries that cross of blame
saviour's crown upon the Son
while she lives in sin.

The apple speaks
of the first quest
the first defiance
the first ostracism

and a bold step
seeking individuality,
an identity self-made

not handed down names,
dressed in pampering —
a pseudonym of dependence

The forbidden fruit
earned a wrath
yet also a home —
a world to make her own.

FRUIT OF KNOWLEDGE

With the first bite
she moved into knowledge
succulently luscious,
giving in to the beckoning
of the forbidden fruit
just within her reach

In a pair of eyes
and half opened t-shirt buttons
sparked passion leashed
in middle class morality —
Thou shalt not be tempted —
chants engraved in mind machinery.

lost virginities, unpreserved chastities
causing blood feuds pickled
in patriarchal sauce —
Far graver than global warming
or the question of human survival
and the fruit of knowledge
is hacked into a thousand atoms.

such unfair compliance
they eyed with annoyance
and loads of defiance

THE WIFE | AYANA

She was a companionate wife
Saree neatly draped around
Her waist, skirting
the rims of her forehead
The stray strand of hair
Betrayed the straying spirit
That roved in abandon
Let loose in times she had
Cherished in untimely dreams
Dreams she had kept to herself

She did certain things and waited
For others to be done
As all was not hers to be done
The saree of course kept her company
The fire surged inside
It had stories to tell
Perfectly embalmed in
Neatly folded closets.

Ayana felt
while going over the spells
now was the time to set the stage
rewrite restore and re-engage

Delusions | Ayana

I hold my world in cupped hands
It trickles down in slipping sands
Those leaves that spring afresh
Soaked in Sapphire sunlight
Flashes of dream drenched memories
Seep through the foliage of shadowy
Deeps.
Painted in receding illusions
Coloured in steaming cups of tea
Words drift in loved insanities
Staging my thoughts in delusions
I hold on to the last sip
Tapping the last dregs of masquerade
Playing my part to the hilt
Conjuring sanity in whispered silence…

Syrma couldn't stay her tongue
it was her turn to strike the gong
take the world by its collar
give it back dime to dollar

THE BLUEBEARD'S ROOM | SYRMA

Mine is a ragpicker's life —
This sack on my shoulders, full of sorrows
I could not bear on brows' other than mine.

In one corner there lie the doubts that plagued
you before that make-or-break meeting
(Surreptitiously taken away,
and replaced with confidence by me).
In another cranny there — the unuttered screams of
the little girl, afraid of the dark.
Here — the pain of that lame puppy,
Carelessly run over by people out to have a 'good' time.
"And behind 'that' door?", you ask —
That locked door you can see in my eyes?
THAT is the land of 'NOUGHT'.
The mask-protecting me
from my own pandemics — for eons now.
Forgotten dates, untended illnesses, successes not celebrated —
Surprises neither given; nor received...
Me befooled, me betrayed, me forgotten.
Some long-ago scars, some still fresh gashes —
Each one shoved hastily,
wriggling and squealing, Behind THAT door.

No ragpickers have yet come knocking — asking for them...
willing to do the clean-up job.
Oh I tried showing them — Once upon a Time...
The dried-up tears, the ashes of desires, the loves unrequited.
But confidences shared — are weaknesses bared.
So now I play along...
Joking about how the most expensive creams
don't lighten the shadows under my eyes —
Totally silent — about what caused them in the first place.
Inside that room, behind That Door...
As the stinking pus of old wounds drains
its poison into the flowing gore of new ones...
Holding on to Yellowing photographs and crumpled memories —
I simply ensure that my Facebook update always reads:
Aj se pehle, aaj se zyada/khushi aaj tak nahi mili...

three battle-weary heads nodded in agreement
even as Ayana had the aunt's miseries to tend

THE (INVISIBLE) AUNT | AYANA

Do I need to explain myself?
Tea/coffee, white/black, with/without sugar
Preferences for the preferred
I love colours when it comes to
Ravishing dresses I adore
Secretly craving their prices to drop
Dropped they have in a clumsy mire of
Fetish and wanton demands
Do I sound like a high priestess in
Crowded slippery bazaars?
It rained in the afternoon
My umbrella refused to budge
Contemptuously it retired in oblivion
It flaunts shades of white and black
I let it go as everything else
My name, my self and my identity
They too have weathered the sun and the storm
Unknowingly holding on to slender undernourished spikes
I thought my explanations were not necessary
But this is what I have been doing
The colour of my skin
The length of my dress
The fire in my womb

Words, words and words
Words inside rooms,
Inside doors, inside walls
I scream, I holler, I speak.

witch Nerissa then recounted her two bits
in their long awaited threesome meet
reality and myth also did meet
boundaries porous travelled indeed

SITA SPEAKS | NERISSA

I am Sita reborn
I leave the comfort of my plush job
Hard earned by years of slog,
The security of a growing bank balance
Replenished every month against my own sweat
The cool and comforting friendships forged over working lunches.
The house that I had fondly nurtured into a home,
Pouring myself into it that it became my extended self
I leave them all.

At your single gesture
I leave them all

I pack myself in suitcases and airbags
Hide behind the fashionable tags of VIP and American tourister
And fly off to a land unknown
Supporting you as you volunteer to take up
Your vanvaas, away from friends and home.
In lands of strange tongues and customs you slog
I keep your home happy and the fire in your kitchen stoked
And wait for the tired you each evening

To prepare you for the next day's battle
You grumble, you complain,
Yet you carry on your vanvaas
At the end of which kingship awaits.

We return at its end
The king in his glory of an inflated purse and a higher throne
And I, his tired, lack lustre wife
Happy to have returned to the left behind home.
Yet could not find the world that was once so own

It did not wait as time dragged on

The king's exile had an expiry, not mine.
It continued like that secret stream
Buried deep within,
Unseen and forgotten by all of its existence.
I remained exiled in my own forests of broken dreams and fractured self.

the globe they did readily embrace
moving through time and space
witches sought their real home
the one they could call their own

THE REAL HOME | NERISSA

Home is where the morning sun peeped
through wooden cracks of eastern window
and baba's voice floated in my sleepy ears
pulling me gently out of dreamless sleep.
The one that I had left twenty six summers back!

But baba said, his home is
that double storeyed building
sheltered by trees —
mango, jackfruit, coconut
and there were so many more.

I was taught that was my home too
An obedient daughter, I tried to learn.

But ma never spoke of HERs!
She spoke of her *jethu's*
the one from which she walked miles
to reach her school
Or her *kaka's*,
the one she got married from,
And then of her husband's
which, who knows

when that became her own!

I learnt and unlearnt addresses
year after year,
home after home,
till I made one
with a room of my own

And now, steep steps frown
as age gathers numbers
upon loved ones all around
and my middle class luxury seeks
an elevator enabled home

Yet each night I thank God,
the roofs had not orphaned my homes,
ever!
Unlike Shanti's or Maya's
for whom the old school building
is the best semblance of a home...

their conversations taking on a new mould

tales of malice now in turns they told
patience pushed to the threshold

enough of tears it's time to fight
injustices new and old

RE-TURNING | AYANA

Pain her only company
Her head steady with last night
Strangely enough those stars
Dimmed by her eyes beckoned
Her feet had found roads less travelled
Not travelled perhaps...
Wading through unwanted thoughts
She suffered the darkness alone
Perhaps waiting for the tunneled light
Silent self-denials met with the
Soft glow of the glow worms
Warmly embracing the sinner
Life had made her lately
Her thoughts wandered groping
For the inner self that had nurtured her
Feebly fettered by that very self
She made her way back
Back in those freshly healed
Waters of life asking her
To dive again in search of
That rare self that kept her afloat

are we just bodies
no self or identities
witches or non-witches
deprived sanctities

ANOTHER GIRL | AYANA

So another girl gets raped and killed
So what?
Many more will suffer the same fate
So what?

Bodies untouchable or not never mattered when touched and tortured
They were merely desired, hated and butchered

Another girl will suffer her lot
Because men will be men

The girl's body is a site of redress
Easy to pin down and shred

Who are these men and where do
They come from?
Is it possible to make them go back
Unlearn what they were taught?

They are the ones who must have
Listened to their mother's lullaby
Or invited reproof
For bunking school
Or ignored their sister's nagging cries
They must have heard their chachi
Summoning them for dinner
Or their mami offering them homemade
Laddus laced with ghee
They must have fetched the doctor
For their ailing dadi, pushed back tears
For someone they held dear.

They must have felt the soft brush
Of youth in intimate stories of love
Or stopped by to hear the next door neighbour's daughter
recite
'Jhansi ki Rani'

When did they turn into
monstrous maniacs
When?

outraged Ayana smouldered in disgust
deceitful gods possessed by lust
fail to uphold women's trust
mirroring the very men
who create them out of dust

Nerissa recounted through myth and folklore
the seething witches couldn't agree more

EVENINGS OF TRANSGRESSION | NERISSA

A slice of evening flickers
In the wick of a fading kerosene lamp
Where soot blankets light
Till nothing more is visible.
On a roadside three bodies lie,
Female mass of flesh.
Like crumpled tissues after feasting orgy.

And they say:
Woman is just her body
Mute soul remains hidden in some corner:
Bodies we are,
Since Eve was first duped
Or even Leda by the Swan
Or Kunti, Draupadi, Amba,
Those women of (so-called) divine interference born,
Transgressed, their wills assaulted, existence denied,
Flesh again in the world of gods and demigods.

The list does not end;
Only Time flies;
Delhi, Kolkata, New York, London
In the mortal world too,
Nameless bodies on roadside cry.

Every evening somewhere,
Soot covers the dying sun
And evening flickers in desperate fear.

as Nerissa paused for breath
Syrma picked up the thread
for when lives are meaninglessly ended
one needs to speak long and hard of death
when such is the shock that eyes forget to cry
words are the only way to bleed the wounds dry

The Revenge | Syrma

They 'used' to lie in wait…
in dark alleys,
near abandoned buildings
beside lonely fields
They 'used' to lie in wait…
For the exhausted 40-something
returning from work,
to swerve into an unfamiliar
short-cut to save a few minutes.
For the excited 20-year-old
walking with her new-found love,
to look for a few stolen moments
of privacy.
For the chirpy six year old playing
with friends,
to come searching for a 'safe'(?)
corner to hide in.
They would wait, watch, measure…
Not the tired gait of the
office-goer
But the roundness of her hips;
Not the twinkling of young eyes
in love,

But the plunge of her neckline;
NOT the peals of childish laughter
But the flesh exposed beneath the
school skirt-hem.

With leering eyes and lolling tongues, they would
measure…
Not persons but bodies…
not the ups and downs of their life stories...
just the swells and curves of breasts and thighs…
And having sized-up
the vital stats (and their helplessness)
They (used to) pounce...
to devour… to tame.

There were many forms to these strippings —
The mental undressing by salivating eyes
The furtively groping hands in a crowded bus
Would become bolder, more familiar,
in those dark alleys, abandoned buildings, lonely fields
tearing at the covering fabrics
impatient to expose flesh.

They STILL lie in wait nowadays...
In lonely hospital morgues
On the banks of the holiest rivers...
For the 40-somethings whose lungs failed them
For the 20 year olds burnt out by fever before any pyre
could.
They are still bodies...still mounds of flesh…
To be hurriedly set afloat ...surreptitiously buried...
Denied a closure...deprived of dignity…
BUT...
The very hands which once craved to gnaw at any sliver of
naked skin

Now shrink away in terror from the slightest touch...
Once a body… even now JUST a body...
But with differences galore...
Once forceful they 'used' to lie in wait…
in dark alleys,
near abandoned buildings
beside lonely fields
They 'used' to lie in wait…
For the exhausted 40-something
returning from work,
to swerve into an unfamiliar
short-cut to save a few minutes.
For the excited 20 year old
walking with her new-found love,
to look for a few stolen moments
of privacy.
For the chirpy six year old playing
with friends,
to come searching for a 'safe'(?)
corner to hide in.
They would wait, watch, measure…
Not the tired gait of the
office-goer
But the roundness of her hips;
Not the twinkling of young eyes
in love,
But the plunge of her neckline;
NOT the peals of childish laughter
But the flesh exposed beneath the
school skirt-hem.

With leering eyes and lolling tongues, they would
measure…
Not persons but bodies…
not the ups-and downs of their life stories…

just the swells and curves of breasts and thighs…
And having sized-up —
the vital stats (and their helplessness)
They (used to) pounce...
to devour… to tame.

There were many forms to these strippings —
The mental undressing by salivating eyes
The furtively groping hands in a crowded bus
Would become bolder, more familiar,
in those dark alleys, abandoned buildings, lonely fields —
tearing at the covering fabrics —
impatient to expose flesh.

They STILL lie in wait nowadays...
In lonely hospital morgues
On the banks of the holiest rivers...
For the 40-somethings whose lungs failed them
For the 20 year olds burnt out by fever before any pyre could.
They are still bodies...still mounds of flesh…
To be hurriedly set afloat...surreptitiously buried...
Denied a closure...deprived of dignity...
BUT...
The very hands which once craved to gnaw at any sliver of naked skin
Now shrink away in terror from the slightest touch...
Once a body…always JUST a body...
Once forcefully exposed, captured...
Now fearfully covered up, shunned...
BUT IN THAT FEAR LIES TRIUMPH...
from being pinned down into immobility
As demonic thrusts rack their innermost crevices
To lying limp, as PPE-clad shadows
rush to shroud them up...

from 'ravishable' to 'untouchable'
is an unenviable journey…
BUT BODIES TOO NEED THEIR REVENGE, you see...

with a heavy heart and a throbbing vein
witch Ayana continued with disdain
adding her link to this chain

LOVE | AYANA

The maggot infested bread
Will give you pimples
Is it reason enough
To reject this bread?
It will not give you
A rumbling stomach
It's okay to get pimples
I thought
A woman's beauty
Is skin deep only
Does it really matter?
A coarse skin or the
Taste of acid that scars
Your skin and soul
You love your skin
I love it too — he said
But his love was strange
It looked through my skin
As the thin red bloody veins
Oozed out in splattered display

not just victims of acid attack
fumed they in livid disgust
foetuses smothered brides were burnt
Ayana agonised in two short songs

VOICES | AYANA

Thud and thump
I am floating
Those machines
They heard me... right?
I aminhererighthere...

Silence
Faint rumblings
I amalone
I a m a l o n e

Noises
You found me
Thank GOD
I love you GOD

Silence
Magical machines
Human hands
Bloodless hearts
I can't breathe
Icantbreatheicantbreathe

BURNT

Cornered walls
Stand tall in busy roads
Burnt to dust

They garbed silken
Dreams, waists carefully draped
Emerald vying with fuchsia
Crimson preferred over jasper
Silk rubbing shoulders with
Jamdani and crepes...
Adored and admired
Never for once relenting
To those craving eyes
The bald mannequins
Endearingly endured
The rallying red
Inflamed in red
Cradled in soot

The bride-to-be
Felt the flames leaping
To be or not to be...

is love to be only oppressive
is love to be just skin deep
why can't it see beyond surfaces
beyond carefully made-up faces

'TRUE LOVE'S KISS' | SYRMA

Scraped Knees,
Bleeding fingers,
(Reminders of the high walls just scaled)...
A red itch spreading angrily across your creamy cheeks —
(Where the 100 year old poison-ivy has scratched your
heretofore unblemished skin)
— You call them Love...
As you swoop into my bed chamber, determined to enjoy
the 'fruits' of all this labour —
Claiming my kisses, even while I lie insensate —
Oblivious to pleasure (or its lack); unable to consent.
You call it Love —
I call it curiosity —
And I call it conquest.

Gnarled fingers, wrinkled hands —
Cleaning cobwebs from ceilings,
Picking the lint out of the linen...
The bent, old figure replacing stained bed-sheets
Changing my soiled clothes —
Trying to ensure that the foul stench of 100 years of
excrement,
Of thousand moons of menstrual blood —

Do not spoil the chances of a sleep-crippled princess's
'happily ever after'.
Continuing to try hard,
even as narratives routinely transmute her legitimate anger
at deprivation into villainy and witchcraft.
Bent double by age (guilt? Righteous rage?), but upright in
intention —
Not extracting revenge, as I lie insensate —
Unable to run, oblivious to care —
You call it Magic?
I call it Love.

cold coffees turning warm
the meet was halfway done

weighing it all in
pensive and grim
the witches went on
dredging time's cauldron

To the Poet | Nerissa

There will be time again
to sing of gulmohars and neem
and the bright periwinkle
winking from the cracked roof
of a house in ruin

There will be time again
to sing that mushy song
of how you had once touched
and each touch a fire
that cruised through my veins

There will be time too
to write paens to a god
who refuses to descend
to the murk of this world
happy in heaven.

Now is not that time.
Now's the time for brand new verse

Sing if you must, of a dying child
of all the tongues tied

Chant if you must, the healing verses
to a race that's dead
write if you must, with your body
the woman that you are
And
For once
Let poetry breathe

and shifted they to lighter play
the day alas was wearing away

food they all cried to say
couldn't be further kept at bay

let's cook it all afresh
spices memories and redress

ROTIS | AYANA

The red palloo
Caressed my back
Yards of desire draped silk
Spread the sky on my shoulders...
I smelt my mother's touch
Her lavender met mine
In swishing pleats
Not matching her expert hands
Placing the red bright bindi
I picked up rotis
Embraced in warmth
Soggy ones nestled in
Her secure sentience
Straight from fire
The sun stepped forth
Edges carefully cooked

Feeling a rush in my throat
I quietly held the burning rims

and once I loved gastronomy
Nerissa sighed with melancholy

FOODIES | NERISSA

Since we met
you have been my
semicolon friend

Not a closure
but a long pause
in the course

of Sunday lunch
a little drool and an
appreciating look

and my tongue is hitched
mind is hooked
and a romance goes on
in the gastronomic lane.

that did call for a hearty laugh
till Ayana sliced some nostalgic stuff

MANGOES | AYANA

Till last year in April
the generous mango tree in my
neighbourhood left us gaping...
at its closely clustered branches.
Mangoes delightfully dripping
with stories laced in juicy memories...
It grew unhindered, claiming space
soulfully, in the wafting fragrance
from my grandmother's kitchen.
Aamkichatni is still my favourite,
lusting at its luscious vernal charm
I held the mangoes close to my bosom,
not letting them slip through
those years of remembrance and forgetting.
This April the mangoes
braved the virulent kalbaishakhi.
They stood tall embodying resilience.
Some of them had relented though,
some braced for the winds in the offing.

nostalgia and dismay
went hand in hand
as Nerissa conjured
some grave strands

MELANCHOLY | NERISSA

The clouded sky
covers my room
in a melancholic shade

From kitchen shelf
l pick up fork
to pluck out sorrows

In old recipe books
I seek potions
to concoct happiness

Yet what's made is a blank stillness
Would you still keep the doors closed?

and they agreed when witches willed
with hearty laughs and throaty squeals
concoct happiness and proudly heal
bruised hearts and cracked heels

REMEDIES | NERISSA

Our hearts healed on the open terrace

Evening breeze
brisk walk
scattered words
tuneless songs —
soothed our claustrophobic ache

In the open kitchen un-modular
conversation locked down for years
broke open sluice gates

Recipes of world
Exotic spices
homegrown love
sauteed melodies
healed some long time bruised hearts.

the witches learnt to weave their dreams
while they cooked washed scrubbed and cleaned

PATTERNS | AYANA

Patterns of soapy lather
rose on unclean dishes.
Those dogged designs
enveloped unseen my
grandmother's wrinkles.
Her hands had scraped
the last dregs of dirt
clinging tenaciously to
her dreams of well crafted
delicacies, so coveted
by her husband and sons.
Those were the patterns
which surreptitiously
made way into my mechanical
movements of rubbing past
those hidden stories...
The greasy oil,
stubborn, stood out,
refusing to disappear
rewriting her dreams of
tales left untold
for her granddaughters.

witches dissented witches conformed
witches had their own motherhood songs
from kitchen to being moms
their adda seamlessly transformed

BIRTH | AYANA

The baby had found its way
The mother still languishing
Her path was bouldered
Uneven and uphill
She waited for the light
Trespassing the tunnel
The roads were crooked
Crooked as the stars
In those blinding nights
Have patience said the others
Just a few more miles
Maybe stretching to some more
Voices poured in
Her eyes had dimmed
With the pain of birth,
And death.

post the birth pang
a mother was born
pean to mothers
was their next song

MOTHER | NERISSA

Mother
Once upon a time
I held your hands
Scared and unaware
Of a world beyond you
Bit by bit
I grew up
Too big to fit into your clasp
Confident of my ways.
Yet you stood by
Quiet, watchful eyes
Guiding from behind
Ever your watchful self

Now that I help
My little one grow
You come back to me
In so many more ways
Grander in motherhood
I look up to your eyes
And can feel my fears
Melt away
Before your caring self.

then Ayana sang aloud
songs verily spun around
her little daughter little no more
growing up for the world in store

My Little Girl | Ayana

My little girl has grown up
Those tiny limbs have responded
To nature's clarion call
The doll house she nurtured
Seeks new residents
New members ask entry
In the dreams which circled
Around my little world
She wishes to be me
With suppressed smiles
I wonder at the travelled miles
Can I bar her from entering
The adult world where dreams
Shed their ethereal garb
Those buds bloom into flowers
Not wary of the humming bird

DAUGHTERS

Her mother gave birth to her
Miracle of sorts
Daughters are not born
They are made
They are made into
Mothers who give birth
The trick is to keep breathing
Breathing life into ideas
To nurture them
As little bodies
Of flesh and blood
Of hope and despair
Bodies with blood
Blood coursing through
Nonchalant veins
Gave birth to some ideas
Those ideas were babies
She held close to her heart
Nurtured them with the
Milk of her thoughts
Which must have fused
The brain and the heart.

Nerissa then thanked
the two little hands
that stayed her rocking boat
at each day's close

OF A MOTHER'S LOVE | NERISSA

As I wrap around your neck
amulet of a mother's love
and sniff in the wisp
of your baby fragrance,
no words flow
yet two hearts beat
in a rhythm known.
In silence I listen
to the falling away
of everyday dust
gathered around my tired heart.
In the breeze that washes over us
I find stories of comfort
and tales of a blind trust.

motherhood was not child's play
for women working at home and away
living up to models of perfection
better be left to works of fiction

DREAMS | AYANA

I often imagine myself as a robot
With a radar picking up signals
From far and wide
The bedroom next to mine
Is my daughter's
She messaged me about
Bed bugs that kept her awake
My dreams too had infiltrators
Warning me of umpteen perils
A scene straight from star wars
The child in me
Felt the pangs of unimpeded violence
Warring stars strewn carelessly
Across the blue ocean sky
Or the rivers emptying themselves
Into the luscious greens
Spewing the fiction behind the real

yet
motherhood is not monochrome
that's what Syrma said
come out of cliches girls
let the boundaries fade

THE TRANSGRESSORS | SYRMA

For a hundred years now- this wait...for one shower of rain,
A hundred years of looking for deliverance from this pain.
Planted in the desert of 'man'— ity,
For a hundred years, I've been searching...for humanity...in vain.

A misfit, because I don't ask creeper-like for shelter,
for support —
A misfit because, oak-like — I invite, I seduce you into my shade.
The roving bee, shining with pollen, comes visiting...
And in a passing encounter
(that was supposed to pass for 'love') — impregnates me.
I feed this being, suddenly implanted within me;
with my very vitality.
And yet...for all my efforts —
the fruit is not for me to take pride in.
I fulfil the ideal of motherhood — I give birth...
But the generations don't carry my name.

If I do not flower for one year, I am 'barren'...
If during a storm,
some of my branches tangle in the foliage of my neighbour —
(as we try to shield the other from the tempest's onslaught) —
I am 'transgressive'...

And my branches are brutally cut —
for the 'man' to move on ahead — "no strings attached".

Time passes as the struggle for survival continues —
Soon the chlorophyll in my leaves loses its greenness —
And almost immediately the manly axe hits mercilessly
at my once-fertile womb.
The brownish sap... blood? gushes out. But no tears, alas!
All seem to have dried up with the milk.

As I fall to the ground with a resigned sigh,
I see the green sapling planted next to me
smile lovingly, as the wind caresses her —
unaware as yet of the demands about to be made.
I wish I could tell her that Dreams are not for us...
I wish I could warn her —
To take undiluted pleasure in the riotous colours of her petals,
the lush velvet of her sepals —
She will have to wait another 100 years —
Like I have!
I wish I could warn her that she is born a 100 years too soon —
Like I Was!

then the three brokered a deal
to talk of passion with some zeal

Love | Nerissa

Silence camouflages the noise
of crumbling walls
that could never be home.
It's not only fuel that chars...

Deep, hidden, lay
a dried well — forgotten,
till the explorer's touch conjured —
and lo! It Overflowed

And there was a new life
fledging its tiny greens
among the grey debris
of burnt down hopes

Yet, what's excavated
tells part of the story —
A bit still lies buried
in dank cells, in dark circles
of old failures and loveless songs

How many Incas are born
when fingers laced in love
wipe away dust
that's centuries old?

of loveless tales centuries old
Syrma had one more to be told
a tale of betrayal of forsaken trust
or maybe with other themes in its folds
hidden beneath the well-known crust

THE DARK LORD | SYRMA

কিছুদিন মনে মনে ঘরের কোণে,শ্যামের পিরিত রাখ গোপনে...[1]

We have all heard of her —
the foolish cowgirl who wagered her heart in the wrong game...
The girl abandoned
By a man too obsessed with the goal of playing 'God'.
Forsaken...
Left to negotiate alone
The world of wagging tongues, taunting fingers, cruel blows...
with floors to wipe, food to cook — AND a husband to please.

শ্যাম কে যখন পড়বে মনে,
চাইবি কালো মেঘের পানে
রান্না শালে কাঁদবি বসে
কাঠ দিয়ে উনুনে[2]

Secret tears, shed and hurriedly dried

1 "kichhudin mone mone ghorer kone" is a traditional Baul song that tries to capture the pain of Radha pining for her Krishna. In the quoted lines, She is being advised to keep her love for Shyam hidden within herself. If and when the separation pangs become too much, she is further advised to mask her tears as ones caused by the damp wood of the kitchen-fire.

2. In these lines taken from the same song as (i) above, Radha is further advised to mask her tears as caused by the damp wood of the kitchen-fire, if and when the separation pangs become too much,..

behind domestic smoke screens,
Tears that generations have wept with her —
Unable as they were, to wipe them away.
Generations have wondered how she dealt with the memories ...
memories of deep embraces, stolen kisses
memories of unending conversations...
when a dark face would look earnestly at her fair one —
and unburden secrets cloudier than his visage..
the secret burdens hidden behind the glory of 'playing' god.
She was- swept away, they say...
by the hypnotic tunes of a practised philanderer's flute.
Swept away — taken — and then forsaken...
But forgotten was she?
Even as the 'man' bartered his heart for heroism's crown,
Even as he lay soaked in the sweat
of the marital bed's duty-bound lovemakings
Did the 'boy' never yearn...
For those lost deep embraces, the stolen kisses...
Those long conversations —
When his long dark face had looked into a devoted fair one —
And unburdened, unfettered, all that pain,
murkier than the storm that had heralded his birth.

Seduced was she by a wandering flute, they say...
A flute that had already carelessly stolen the hearts of millions,
they point out...
But they also admit that —
this flute never played another note, once their paths diverged...

A mere mortal girl, lusted after by a god, and then forsaken...
Should have been turned to stone, as Ahalya reminds us...
But *this* girl earned her place in temples and in posterity's hearts —
Was this the Dark Lord's final gift then?
this taking on of the blame of being the 'demon' lover,

the unfeeling one... 'the one who left'...
Staking in posterity, the very grandeur he had once
abandoned her for...
Is this his olive-branch, sheepishly offered?
The immortal God opening himself to
centuries of accusing tongues
to compensate for the ones he left her to face —
even in worship, accepting the blame —
'বনমালী তুমি পর জনমে হোয়েও রাধা'[3]
After all, Mortal or God- मर्द को दर्द नहीं होना चाहिए ज़्यादा...[4]
Even if the heart smoulders drier than
the most rocky hammada[5].

---

3 *Bonomali tumi poro jonome hoyo Radha* is another very well known folk song in which Radhika is heard wishing that Krishna is born as her in his next life, as only then would he be able to comprehend the depth of her love and suffering.

4 *mard ko dard nahi hota* is the hindi counterpart of 'Boys Don't Cry', the toxic cultural conditioning of patriarchy that has, and continues to, rob men from acknowledging their legitimate feelings and vulnerability.

5 'hammada' is a word of Arabic origin, meaning an arid rock-strewn desert region.

but why sing of love
solely in notes of grief and pain
listen to a song now
in passionate strain

PASSION | NERISSA

Like a butter softened dough
she found herself fit
right into the cradle
of those arms
where for days
she had deposited
all her yearnings,
all her fancies
and turned them into
whisperings of nothing
that nibble bit by bit
the small of those ears.
Flattened upon that chest
like the perfect circle of roti
she rose up to the lips
and found her way
running deeper,
salivating desires
all the way down the lane
And then,
in the heat that rose upwards
she lost herself forever
baked into
a naked slice of
passion unadulterated

witch Nerissa had set the tone
for matters carnal and forlorn
when it's love to witches much is known
Syrma however had a different tone

THE SIN | SYRMA

I have wiped away your kisses,
As one does incriminating fingerprints.
Locked away your name
Like an accomplice one wants to save.
I am on the run from your memories
As if from that still-warm corpse...
Which just a few minutes ago was a Life.

Every sign of my love for you
I hide inside me...
As if- it is my most brutal crime —
Secret, never to be talked about,
But Always, gnawing at the thoughts...

I hide it, for that's the way it should be...
And yet — like a sliver of the murderer's flesh
Caught beneath the clawing nails of the quivering victim,
Desperately fighting to break the stranglehold...
My gaze keeps flitting back to your face
Hypnotised, fascinated, as it were, by its own capability for darkness.
Run...why don't I run?
Do I then hope...someone will notice, recognise and make the revealing call?
Are you then the Sin, for which —
I WANT to take the Fall?

Ayana tuned in with buried memories
wishing to outgrow her lost fantasies

WISHES | AYANA

The light streams in, mixed with rain-washed green.
These echo in plaintive songs of pulsating blues, reds, and colourless hues.
Resonances of laughter amidst lost memories cavorting to magical tunes.
How is the light visible in darkness undefined? Does it wear lurid costumes or does it stoop in bruised burdens of forgotten dreams?

I seek your ever-present body embracing my soulless soul.
I seek your tremors in quiet noons of proliferating disgust.
I have levelled my pains with tales of slipping delights.
Holding my mundane present in those futureless songs of potent decline. Send me your wishes if you still have them

then she spoke of taboos galore
women's bodies invite allure
opinions shift from goddess to whore
let's sift reality from the dated lores

MY BLOOD | AYANA

My blood scares you
Or is it necessary defilement
You could wish away
A dark secret that
Visited lady Macbeth
Coaxing blood-smeared bonds

My blood incites you
Or is it necessary sinning
In silence whispered
In hushed breaths
Speaking of unspeakable truths
When desires speak unwanted

My blood singes you
Or is it a necessary oasis
In this deserted wasteland
It speaks in red
The colour of my passions
Ignited in wondrous hues

My blood transforms you
Remaking your placid desires
Transfusing your godless soul
Gods see your indifference
But you can't...
This blood runs through
My body and soul

many-hued are words and their connotations
cause for mourning as well as celebrations
talking of body soul and blood
hence unlocked a different kind of flood

how could one ignore for long
the greatest inspiration of most songs

don't forget love in quarantine
the ache and balm of that terrible time

Quarantined Love | Nerissa

Quiet keyboard taps its way into flat screen of a neonatal blue
leaving trail like those postpartum stretch marks
writing new poems on the once blank skin.

Somewhere in two cities postmodern couples in estranged
lands bond over sleek gadgets and weekend domesticity.

Web overflows in soundless conversations;
a word-wrapped universe
explodes in trafficking emotions
across borders in a seamless transference.

Multi sized keyboards tap away,
in an unstoppable zeal of jingoists,
to churn out letter by letter — squeezed emotions from dry hearts
like a toothpaste tube flattened upon a stale hospitality.

Yet somewhere blooms the dahlias and lilies in a small
patch of ground meticulously watered in this virtual world
where truth comes coloured in many realities.

words had always been elusive
when it came to birthing creative
they never added up to the known
witches grafted new saplings to be sown

SPACES | NERISSA

In the space between words
lie thoughts...
How much effort
does it take
to move from one
to the next?

The white space carries
the burden of it all —
craziness, idiosyncrasies,
uncertainties, insecurities,
the mark of gender disparities
the sweat of an artist
or an inner call.

These spaces are pauses
too active to be seen
too fragile to be shared;
and in the pause
are born the words
that speak much more
than the obvious.

In between,
lie a thousand journeys
folded within
the unrevealed.

What's unsaid, weighs
more than those
black marks upon white.
Drudgery of penning
camouflaged in the
flourishing letters
unconfined.

BLANK | AYANA

Blank spaces
Glare back
Some words
None perhaps
Float in poise
These are the ones
Which were written
Forever
Or never.
Emptiness is it?
Or is it rumblings
Of a trapped spirit
Blank to the core
Sending signals
In void.

hope and despair
quiet and chaos
in varied colours emerge

nature and nurture
in Ayana's next venture
find their paths converge

GREEN | AYANA

A patch of green
Longingly lingers
On the fringes though
Ready to claim turf
Last year
The pale brown
Held it back
Like tea-stains
Never letting it go
Making rains disappear
Like the sun in rains
The rains have
Made it again
Coaxing cloudy seams
Slush they come
Splashing forth
Enticing new colours
(Monochromatic)

The foliage is green
A safe haven for
The vanishing hues
Vanishing dreams

Dreamy heads
Headless dreams
Soundless screams
Drumming dreams
DRUMMM...DRUMMzzz
Echo in the vast abyss
Feeding quiet into chaos
And Chaos into quiet...

PEACE | AYANA

I don't know why
when I think of peace
I think of dew drops
Silently resting on
Morning green
Bubbles frothing on
Cold silent waters
Trees fading in
The dim setting sun
Rainbow waiting restlessly
To disappear in azure blue
Chrysalis making its way
To coloured transits
Mountains peeping over
Limitless horizons
Oceans churning lost
Blue-eyed tales

And the clock
Ticking a timely good bye

do not be fooled by a nature benign
in a blink she can change to foul from fine
if we keep crossing our lines

A DAY AFTER AMPHAN | NERISSA

The road so oft taken
lay claimed by foliage
a mass of dense green
dark, damp, dying,
foreboding and grimacing.

The city gasped for some fresh air that morning!

Like resurrected ghosts
half spoken promises,
and whispered hopes
wandered along these streets
like lost souls in a quest for the known

The city too needed some resurrecting!

A colourful kite, rudderless
hung from one of the fallen branches
still carrying smiles
from an innocent childhood
lost perhaps in the mayhem
of the unleashed uncertainties.

the sky had turned grey
reminding them of delay
gossips had matured
so had they

The Sky | Ayana

Then the sky burst
In thousand tears
Oblivious...
To blazing bludgeon
Of furious flaming furnace
Blissfully ignorant
Of parched cries
Blooming buds
Restlessly resting birds
Deaf...
To strained rhapsodies
Resonating with solitude

Then the sky burst
In thousand smiles
Infant seeds queued
For the elixir of life
In raptures infinite
Joyous amplitude
Whispered breaths...
New life springs
In delirious delight.

wrinkles crowfeet saggy skin
all for the cauldron lined in
age gender appearance
out they went for a pittance
tapped they in gleeful dance
melting all with a magical glance

CRISP FORTY | NERISSA

Across the magic threshold,
                    I felt lighter
Stares or words stuck no more
to a surface grown slippery —
accumulated years of slimy blabbering,
had waxed my skin to a polished gleam!

It took two score springs
to be liberated truly —

from your high browed criticism
or snooty nosed disdain
or the whisperings
that once melted self esteem,
a diluted trickle of a sloppy stream.

Two scores it took
to love the sagging breasts
and the untoned flesh,
greying buns and cobwebs
playing around baggy eyes:
parts unconditionally mine!
Parts — anathema to your commercial sight
fed by a plastic media
and its chauvinist snides.

Two scores later
Sleeveless wardrobe and skimpy,
BUT
for my comfort seeking body
in the tropical summers of sultry heat
not for the roving you, oh please!
    And flat heels to comfort my aging soles
    Alice, Angelou food for soul.

Two scores years yet again
to shape my desires — to match my flow
I do not care now, NOW that I know —
I have unclipped my wings
some forty suns late
Yet the full road, I dare to go!

Ayana still had her inhibitions
age and death lurked in her visions
stereotypes loomed large
witches too struggled for charge

My Shadow | Ayana

Looking out of the mirror
She stands arms akimbo
With arched eyebrows
Resting uneasily on those jaded eyes
She falters in her smiles
Pale listless teeth prising limpid lips
Those crinkled cheeks
Slipping past the bones
The aged folds enfolding crevices unseen

How have you been doing?
Comes the familiar flourish
Have you made the mark?
Have you outgrown those endless...
I stop her short
Don't remind me I say
Grey hairs look triumphantly askew

A slight stoop and a gouty recline
I am all alone I say
You must have lost your way
Go! Go! Never come again another day
With an invincible smirk
She recedes like an ever-present shadow
Free from invisible lights
Lurking in those unsettling insights

VERSIONS OF DEATH | AYANA

Our version of death
Clashes with theirs
Some define it as
An unseen presence
Some of course can
See and feel it everyday
Some confront it in
Nightmares seen in
broad daylight
My own versions
Have been frivolous
At times grossly so...
I am alive and everyday
I inch towards it
Laughing at its insipidity
Nameless and impossibly
Grave, it beseeches me
To disentangle its mysterious lurch
Dark and disingenuous
It's not a poet's fathomless
Metaphor, politely scripted to
Touch our hearts in moments of
Respite...

It lurks everywhere
In the screened smirks
Of disoriented dismissals
In the sleepless nights of
Sleeping to rejuvenate
In the half-hearted cries
Of the old beggar woman
Who grudgingly disappeared

breaking down the set constructs
they forged their own forms
with their magic charm they tried
to weed out patriarchal norms

WOMAN/ SELF/ I | NERISSA

I plucked out phrases
from each language
words patriarchal
their hefty baggage.
I sifted through them
picked and chose
those words that suit
my body and pose.

Talk not like that,
Nor sit anymore
Why do you laze
Who will do your chores.

Plenty of these
I weeded out in glee
those that were left
them I moulded for me

Yes I shall work
get my fingers burnt
let sun tan my face
In rains I shall dance

I burn my bridges
I sully my name
My idol I choose
the Scarlet Woman

Let my skin sag
my eyes get baggy
Clothes xxl or
All looks full shabby

What do I care
Why should I
Not Angels for me,
Let witches there be.

and then she remembered
a love gone sour
the day she stepped out of
her good girl's bower

WAYS OF LOVE | NERISSA

Once I had loved
In the only way I knew
femininity charms
taught since nursery days
with the serving heart
nurtured under woman's skin
with the Tutoring Unquestioned
conditioned to 'always' give away
In an unconditional, muted gesture…
Love for me meant just that way.

But somewhere while
walking along the maze of life,
unlearning all those years
I learnt to unburden
the load of expectations
harnessed to womanly shoulders
When I unleashed my free self to create her own sea of desires
I did not un-love you

That was when love was, like never before
When I loved you in spite of

Yet That was when
you chose to walk away
from my newly born self
Scared of its freedom's dazzling brilliance
That was when you felt threatened
by the real me, free of my shackles,
Stripped off years of cultural bondage
It was in these moments
Eve has been forever witch hunted

Syrma huffed and puffed
should the boys have all the fun
walking away isn't just their game
beware it won't long remain the same

The Exit Clause | Syrma

Forever is a heavy burden to bear...
Not because you may stop loving me —
But because I may stop to care...
You are not a fairy tale, but maybe soon that won't bother —
For I will no longer be the coffined Princess
Whom happily ever after can smother.

Every time my hands reach out
And do not find your finger tips...
Every time my kisses come back
Without touching your lips...
I blanche with inexplicable fears.
Not because you just broke my heart again,
But 'coz — one day — I may break yours.

Your betrayals are on your conscience
Only my frailties on mine...

For, my Love, you see —
Rivers dry up... change their course
That does not surprise anymore —
But the last time an ocean bared her sand — papered soul
It became the stuff of legend, of lore.

Replacing a thin filament is enough
To re-light a Fuse...
When the pulsating Vesuvius cools —
Now, THAT is News.

Be the passionate gale if you want a raging fire...
Nature cannot tolerate Vacuum —
And I won't fight Physics for you —
So, Every time you bruise my heart —
By not following promises through...
I am afraid... you lose the 'Goddess'
In not giving the 'Devil' her due.

we shall not
we will not
take the beaten road
shoes fit
or unfit
we'll carve a path
of our own

JOURNEY | AYANA

Those shoes you wore
Were misfits
It's time to try new ones
You have worn them
On those bouldered paths
Where the grass looked
Green on the other side
Those trees stood still
Casting lean shadows
On those patchy pavements
It's time to try new ones
When your dreams outgrow
Those soulless seams

Do you look for them in your father's rack
Or do you spend a thousand breaths
Holding eternity like slipping sands
They remain elusive, alluring you
To travel shoeless that extra mile...
Fasten those shoestrings and look sharp
Maybe you find them lying forbidden
In cloudy maze of lost desires
Maybe you suffer in ignorance
Sadly denying their silent presence...

before witchy tales come to close
remember witches are not bores
they know how to have fun
till their life's race is run
to take away what's their due
their cauldron bubbles with strength anew

LOCKDOWN WOMEN @ 10PM | NERISSA

Finally, 10pm is here
The house at last is calm and quiet
and my workstation beckons
I forget me the wife or mom
sister, daughter, real or in law
it's me, my phone and laptop now

A friend in wait, hello how are you
or paper writing, book review
or a movie that waits to be seen
some songs long in the queue
poems in pipeline to be read
whatever I do, I command my wish.

Nose deep in a book much loved
or scribbling rhymes in pages rough
texts exchanged in between too
with those who now stay separate
yet living in mind and online
ten pm brings them all alive

Lock me down, O lockdown
bind me to the daily grill

make my home my workplace too
and saddle me with householding
through the day if I mop and cook
Ten pm be my Xanadu.

If morning chores frown on me
eggs me on to the bed
warns of dire consequences
of a droopy morning ahead
who cares! Not I, ten pm calls
the magic mantra to survive

Ten pm be my breathing space
my little Island of sanity
absolved of all expectations
all my womanly duties.
Oh ten pm can you conjure
From so many selves, the real me?

like the erstwhile poet's forlorn
10 pm rang a bell before long
the witches had another life of travails
that waited to engulf without fail
pulling on the customary masks
that both a pandemic and patriarchy asks

the threesome said their adieus
drawing the adda to a reluctant close
with the promise to meet again
thunder lightning or in rain
and pour their hearts out unrestrained
for the witches tales need to go on
rising like the phoenix's song

THE MAKING OF THE SONGS

Magic and subterfuge have almost always gone hand in hand. So when three outwardly, if deceptively, calm matrons decided to collaborate for artistic purposes, pretty soon they metamorphosed into witches who seamlessly fitted into this creative pastiche. Witches who dared to weave magic with words. Words that question, defy, restore, rewrite. Witches who revelled in their differences as much as their resemblances. It was all about not writing the 'right' things and we surprised each other by making the same mistakes and telling the same stories. We inhabited our cocoon of secrets, before witnessing its gradual expansion into a world of shared experiences. We often ended up cracking old chests of memories, revisiting long-lost dreams. We forged and planned, waited and stated, agonised and parried but never for once not believe in our witchy enterprise. We were readily — at times unconsciously — taking strides across boundaries of time, space, and language reclaiming female voices both mythical and real. Negotiating hardened patriarchal codes was exhilarating and enervating as some of the poems forced us to think and rethink the deeply ingrained power dynamics. Words are probably the last bit of magic left in this singularly unmagical world, and this gift of words, sometimes diffident and uncertain, sometimes confident and loud, gave us the power to indulge in our deepest thoughts. The gift of magic allowed us to indulge in wishful thinking: wish our dialogues bring redemption, wish they transform the rules of the game. This — needless to say — draws on a long tradition of feminist questioning, critiquing and reworking of patriarchal codes, and a deliberate donning of rebellious nonchalance.

The poems fitted like the pieces of a jigsaw puzzle, reminding us of the subterranean conditioning we as women had undergone. Often the images bled into each other standing in for one another. Repeated readings and discussions made our pieces alive, receptive, and amenable to new interpretations. The pandemic had kept us apart but we kept meeting through mindscape portals, made possible via the emotional and intellectual conduits we had forged in our collective threesome unconscious. Listening, reading, opining, revising, and above all exploring each other's thoughts and ideas, was akin to feeling bonded and unfettered like never before. The nosy witch, the sexy witch, the madcap witch, the belligerent witch, the bitchy witch all partook of our delightful escapades. And we found ourselves exchanging shoes, some ill-fitting, some nearly perfect.

PRAISE FOR THE WITCHES

Then came the Pandemic, the lockdown, the opening up of virtual spaces... and they chose to abandon their matronly demeanour and become errant! ... and, of course, they had the virtual coffee house to meet and chat... on their broomsticks, they travelled across lands, seas, rivers, across time and space...

Three women turn themselves into witches and wield their pen instead of broomsticks. Or, is the pen their broomsticks to clean up the cobwebs of apparently innocuous patriarchal narratives? And they do it with such elan! With the witches' uninhibited glee, they sing delightful songs, write verses while re-cooking, pickling multicultural myths, reality, stories and felt experiences into their cauldron and garnishing them with 'matriarchal spices' and serving with 'feminist sauce.'

Here is a new genre of (Coffee) Table Talk that fuses apparent irreverence with political innocence, mixes earnestness and play, and re-tells in varying styles, mood and attitude of the three narrators. The most absurdly profound question of Icarus' sister, why wasn't the feathers of her brother stitched, instead of sticking them together with wax, that could have prevented the fall, is the essence of the politically disengaged common sense view of things that has a redemptive potential. *Three Witches' Songs* is sure to convince the discerning reader, of Gabriella Herstick's words, that, '(b)eing a witch means living in this world consciously, powerfully and unapologetically.'

JHARNA SANYAL

Three Witches' Songs is a tongue-in-cheek de-stereotyping of gender identity and gender roles, mixed, shaken and stirred with the sorcessors' elan and creative chic. So 'Ayana, Nerissa, and Syrma call themselves Aparna, Nabanita, and Sudeshna in another world.' But in the bewitching intimate world of their own, the three witches are rhymesters, poets, playmates and influencers, often upset with the inequalities of life experiences. Their songs are often a caveat, their songs express concern and care, their songs are about stress and distress. These enchanting songs of the three poet-witches, represent life in all its colours and countless shades, from grey and charcoal to red and black. So the songs of the three witches declare their uniqueness. unequivocally — 'Now's the time for brand new verse.'

SANJUKTA DASGUPTA

GRACIAS

Witches expressing gratitude perhaps goes against most stereotypes entrenched in public consciousness. And like most stereotypes, one that we refuse to let circumscribe us.

Aparna, Nabanita, and Sudeshna; as we call ourselves in the mundane world, owe a lot to a lot of people, who we could trust enough to lay bare our witchy selves (and the unpolished,tentative yieldings of our quills). And despite their busy schedules and varied commitments, the way they encouraged our flights-of-fancy and words, if not on actual broomsticks; has left us feeling overwhelmed and very thankful.

Dr. Nabina Das has given our poems a foreword that grasps the very essence of our intents, and expressed it in her characteristic cogent, lucid way. Professor Sanjukta Dasgupta, Professor Jharna Sanyal, Professor Malashri Lal put pause to their own creative pursuits, to not only read through our manuscript, but also have penned encouraging words for these former students of theirs (witches though they may have morphed into).

The young illustrator, Abhishek Maity, painstakingly decoded our, often garbled, instructions to provide us with illustrations that form apt companion pieces to our words. Kiriti Sengupta and Bitan Chakraborty broke all patriarchal stereotypes, and agreed to give voice (read-print) to our rebellious selves; and we thank them and the whole team of Hawakal; for letting the cauldron come to a boil, and the book to reach the readers.

Talking of readers, we are grateful to Soumi Duttagupta and Subhajit Sengupta— two of our earliest readers for their time and feedback.

All three of us would also like to thank our friends and family, for bearing the brunt of our witchy selves good-naturedly (sometimes just exhausted- and resignedly). Just by letting us be, they have given us a lot to be thankful for.

A few of our evocations, included here, had been previously published in anthologies like *Voices and Vision*, *Hibiscus: poems that heal & empower*, *Yearbook of Indian Poetry in English*, and in e-zines like *SETU*, and *Different Truths*. Our thanks to them too.

DR APARNA SINGH is an Assistant professor of English in Diamond Harbour Women's University. She has taught in various educational institutions across Kolkata in the last decade. Her area of interest includes Indian Writing in English and Dalit Literature. She has published in various national and international journals till date. She has four edited volumes to her credit and has worked as a copyeditor with Sahitya Akademi.

A translator and creative writer, NABANITA SENGUPTA holds a PhD in English and is an Assistant Professor of English in Kolkata. She has translated *A Bengali Lady in England* (Shambhabi), and *Chambal Revisited* (Hawakal), co-edited a volume of critical essays *Understanding Women's Experiences of Displacement* (Routledge) and a poetry anthology *Voices and Vision* (Virasat). She has also authored an e-book of fiction, *The Ghumi Days* (Juggernaut). Nabanita Sengupta has been variously published in journals, anthologies and e-zines. She is the executive committee member of Intercultural Poetry and Performance Library, Kolkata.

DR SUDESHNA CHAKRAVORTY is currently Assistant professor, and Head of the Department of English, Sushil Kar College (affiliated to Calcutta University); and also serving as Guest Faculty in the Post Graduate section of the departments of English, Lady Brabourne College, and St. Paul's Cathedral Mission College, Kolkata. Her areas of interest include Gender Studies, Folklore and Culture Studies; and she has presented papers in several national and international conferences, and published articles on topics related to these areas.